MEAN MACHINES
BOATS

MARK MORRIS

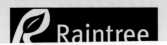
Raintree

For information, address the publisher:
Raintree, 100 N. LaSalle, Suite 1200, Chicago, IL 60602

Customer Service: 888-363-4266
Visit our website at www.raintreelibrary.com

Printed and bound in China by South China Printing Company.
09 08 07 06 05
10 9 8 7 6 5 4 3 2 1

Library of Congress Cataloging-in-Publication Data:

Morris, Mark, 1965-
   Boats / Mark Morris.
      p. cm. -- (Mean machines)
   Includes bibliographical references and index.
   ISBN 1-4109-0557-8 (library binding - hardcover) -- ISBN 1-4109-0831-3 (pbk.) 1. Ships--Juvenile literature. 2. Boats and boating--Juvenile literature. I. Title. II. Series.
   VM150.M665 2004
   623.82--dc22
                                2004014133

Acknowledgments
Aker Finnyards p. 41 (top); Art Directors and Trip pp. 32, 40; Boeing pp. 16–17, 50, 50–51, 51; Corbis pp. 4–5 (Neil Rabinowitz), 5 (middle) (Patrick Ward), 6 (Ludovic Maisant), 7 (Yogi.Inc), 10 (bot) (Bettman), 12 (top) (Hulton Getty), 13, 17, 20 (top), 24, 27, 28 (Yogi.Inc), 30–31 (Patrick Ward), 31, 41 (Chris Rainier), 42 (Bettman) 43 (Sygma), 44 (top) (Lowell Georgia), 44 (bot) (Neil Rabinowitz), 49, 54, 54–55 (Najlay Feanny), 55, 57(Amos Nachaum), Fastship p.57; Hovercraft International p. 34; Hulton-Getty pp. 5 (bot), 10 (top), 16, 25, 28–29, 34, 48 Kockums p. 23; Lockheed-Martin pp. 5 (top), 22; Maritime Museum pp. 8, 8 (top), 11; Mary Evans Picture Library pp. 14, 14–15; PA Photos pp. 12, 15, 32, 33, 35, 45, 47, 48–49; PPL pp. 36, 37, 38, 46; Rex Features pp. 39, 42; Science Photo Library pp. 25 (top), 26, 30; SOVFOTO pp. 52–53, 53; Sylvia Cordaiy Picture Library 108969 p. 3 United States Navy pp. 6, 18, 18 (top), 20, 21; VRI p. 38 (top).

CONTENTS

Any words appearing in the text in bold,
like this, are explained in the glossary.
You can also look out for them in the "Up To
Speed" box at the bottom of each page.

THE WORLD OF BOATS

SEE FOR YOURSELF

Many famous ships are still thrilling passengers long after their traveling days are over. They are turned into floating museums, and the public can go on board and tour them.

Welcome to the amazing world of boats. The best boats do not just go fast, they go the fastest. They do not just dive under water, they dive the deepest. They have more sails, more engines, more power. They are the biggest, the heaviest, the most expensive, or the very first to achieve something.

Boats come in many different shapes and sizes. The only thing they have in common is the water.
- Some dive underneath it.
- Some cut straight through it.
- Some skim across the surface.

But they all make the best use of it.

WHERE ARE THEY?

So where should you go to see boats? Good sense tells us that water is the best place. So keep your eyes open near the **coast.** Take a closer look at the ships in ports and harbors. Or see if there is a large lake near you that has a sailing club.

Another excellent place to see amazing boats is at a museum. In fact, many boats are museums themselves. You can go on board and take a look around. There is information everywhere, and tour guides will tell you anything you want to know.

FIND OUT LATER . . .

Which boat is the most difficult to see?

Which boat needs miles to stop?

Which boat dives the deepest?

Speedboats like this are toys for the rich and famous.

WN1384RA

5

THE SHIPPING STORY

What turns an ordinary boat into an amazing boat? Is it speed or is it size? Must it be a record breaker? Does it have to be modern?

It could be all of these things or none of them. It is likely that the greatest boats will have something special that makes them different from the others.

Perhaps they can dive the deepest, or maybe they are the heaviest, largest, fastest, or weirdest. Many of the boats that people think are the best can be found in this book.

BUILT FOR BATTLE

Nimitz-class aircraft carriers are the largest warships afloat. They have over 5,500 **crew** and cost around $5 billion to build. They are over 1,083 ft (330 m) long, carry 85 aircraft, and are powered by two nuclear reactors. They are huge!

TECH TALK

Royal Clipper: technical data
- **Masts**: 5
- **Length**: 469.2 ft (143 m)
- **Width**: 54.1 ft (16.5 m)
- **Weight**: 5,510 tons
- **Crew**: 105
- **Maximum mast height**: 197 ft (60 m)

If the sea looks too cold, the *Royal Clipper* has three onboard swimming pools!

crew   group of people that works on a boat or ship
mast   upright pole to which sails are attached

OLD MEETS NEW

The most amazing boats do not always have to be the most modern. There are many different ways to travel the oceans, after all.

The *Royal Clipper* is the world's largest sailing ship. This ship mixes modern luxury and old-fashioned, romantic charm.

Sails are not computer-operated on the *Royal Clipper*. Skilled **sailors** do the work by hand, just as they did in the old days. But the ship is built from modern materials.

UNDERWATER GIANT

This Russian Typhoon-class **submarine** is the largest sub ever built. It is 564 ft (172 m) long and has a crew of 160. It can reach 29 mph (46 km/h) under water and can go 1,312 ft (400 m) deep.

sailor member of a ship's crew
submarine ship that can travel under water

WIND POWER

Sailing uses the power of moving air to push a boat through water. People learned how to use the wind to move their boats thousands of years ago.

ANCIENT POWER

The oldest picture of a sail is from Egypt. It is nearly 8,000 years old. It was a simple square sail. These can still be seen on sailing ships today. Sails allowed the ancient Greeks and Romans to build great trading ships. Viking longships also had sails. Over the years, people learned how to make better sails. Having good sailing ships meant that a country could trade and fight successfully.

SAIL SPEED

Clipper ships were fast sailing **vessels** built to carry **cargo**. Two of the most famous are the *Cutty Sark* and the *Thermopylae*. Both ships broke speed records in the 1800s. The *Thermopylae*, pictured above, was destroyed in 1907. The *Cutty Sark* is now a museum and has attracted more than fifteen million visitors.

HMS *Victory* was one of the most powerful sailing ships.

cargo   goods carried by a ship
dry dock   place where boats can be kept out of water

RULING THE WAVES

The British were very powerful in the 1700s and 1800s. A major reason for this was their excellent ships. HMS *Victory* was a huge, powerful gun platform that could sink any of its enemies.

Admiral Lord Nelson died on board *Victory* at the Battle of Trafalgar in 1805. *Victory* was retired in 1812. Today it is in a **dry dock** at Portsmouth, England. It attracts half a million visitors every year.

CLIPPER ROUTES

Clippers were first built to carry tea from China. They were forced to find other ways to earn money when steamships became more advanced (see page 10). This was because steamships could travel in any weather and did not need the wind. Clippers also carried coal from South America and wool from Australia.

TECH TALK

HMS *Victory*: technical data
- Length: 226.4 ft (69 m)
- Width: 51.5 ft (15.7 m)
- Depth: 23 ft (7 m)
- Highest **mast**: 204.7 ft (62.4 m)
- Number of sails: 37
- Top speed: 12 mph (19 km/h)
- Number of guns: 104
- Crew: 821

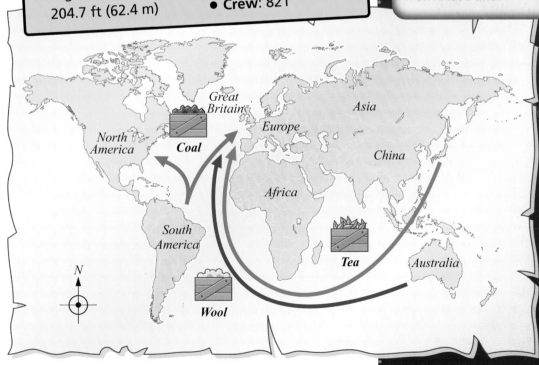

STEAM AND SPEED

During the 1800s, steam engines began to take the place of wind and sail power. Many inventors and engineers tried to find new mechanical ways of using steam to power ships.

PADDLE POWER

The first big change was the invention of the paddlewheel. When these huge wheels turned, the wide, flat blades dipped into the water and pushed the boat along.

BELOW DECKS

In the engine room, a coal fire heated water to produce steam. The steam ran through pipes to an engine. The steam forced a **piston** to move in and out of a **cylinder** in the engine. This piston was attached to a **crankshaft** that turned the paddlewheel.

STORMING SIRIUS

In 1838 the English paddle steamer *Sirius* was the first ship to cross the Atlantic Ocean using just steam power. It was the first ship to make the crossing without using a sail.

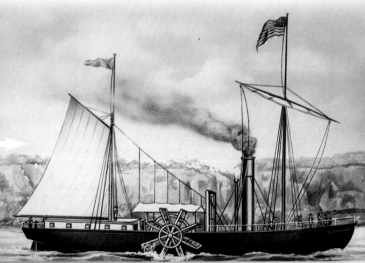

The *Clermont* could easily carry up to 100 passengers.

crankshaft   part of an engine that is joined to the pistons
cylinder   tube-shaped part of engine in which fuel is burned

TICKET TO RIDE

Paddle steamers were soon being used all over the world. They were very good on calm water such as lakes and rivers.

In 1807 the first successful steamboat company offered regular trips up and down the Hudson River between New York City and Albany, New York.

The journey was made on the steamboat *Clermont*, built by the inventor Robert Fulton. His boat could make the 150-mile (240-kilometer) trip in 32 hours, with an average speed of around 5 miles per hour (8 kilometers per hour).

The idea soon caught on. Paddle steamers began chugging up and down rivers all over the world. The most famous were the luxury steamers of the Mississippi River. These steamers are still going strong today.

PROPELLERS FOR THE SEA

When it was built in 1843, the SS *Great Britain* was the largest ship afloat. It was designed by the famous engineer Isambard Kingdom Brunel and was the first **propeller** ship designed for the ocean. A propeller shipmoves using a set of underwater blades. These blades are spun around by the steam engine to produce movement.

In 1861 the SS *GreatBritain* transported an English sports team to tour Australia.

piston part of engine that slides in and out of a cylinder
propeller part of a ship's engine that spins under water and drives the ship along

BUILDING A SHIP

Many people are involved in building a ship. **Welders**, engineers, electricians, plumbers, carpenters, painters, **riveters,** and blacksmiths all play their part in preparing a ship for the sea.

SHIPBUILDING YARDS

A hundred years ago, shipbuilding yards were common around the **coast.** Even when metal replaced wood as the main building material, people carried on building ships in much the same way. The "skeleton" of the ship was put together first, and then metal plates were riveted to it, just like the planks used in a wooden craft.

When it was finished, the ship was launched by smashing a wine bottle over the **bow.**

I NAME THIS SHIP . . .

The launch of a new ship is a spectacular and exciting event. Many people turn up to watch monster supertankers slide down into the water.

assembly   putting together different parts
bow   front end of a boat or ship

MODERN TIMES

These days, there are far fewer shipbuilding yards. Ships are no longer the only way to move **cargo** and people around the world.

Computers are used in today's shipbuilding. Many jobs, such as metal plate-cutting and **assembly,** are now done by robot workers. Ships are built in sections and are only brought to the dock for assembly. When a ship is launched today, it is often as an empty floating shell. The work of assembling the inside of the ship begins when it is actually afloat.

SIDEWAYS SLIDE

Some ships, like this **submarine,** are launched sideways into the water. This method creates a huge splash and is usually done when space in the harbor is limited.

---

rivet   short metal pin that fixes sheets of metal together
welder   person who joins pieces of metal by melting the edges

LUXURY LINERS

A **liner** was a special ship, built to carry large numbers of passengers across the Atlantic and Pacific oceans. The ships were as luxurious as the best hotels. Only the very rich could afford the luxury. For most passengers, the cabins were very small and crowded.

The golden age of the liner was during the 1920s and 1930s. There was great competition between the shipping companies to provide the fastest service. The **Blue Riband** was an award for the fastest ship to cross the Atlantic. The fastest ship would become famous and get more passengers or **cargo.**

The *Queen Mary* completed 1,001 Atlantic crossings.

DEATH OF THE FLOATING PALACES

By the 1950s jet aircraft were able to cross the oceans much more quickly than ships. The great luxury liners could not compete and stopped running. Only a very small number are still running today.

HALES TROPHY

Harold Hales introduced the Hales Trophy in 1933. This is now awarded to the holder of the Blue Riband.

CAT-POWER

In 1998 the Blue Riband was awarded to a Danish super ship, *Catlink IV* (below). This ship managed an average speed of 47.5 mph (76 km/h) on the journey across the Atlantic.

>>>>>>>>>>>>
Find out more about the history of the Blue Riband on page 59.

WAR AT SEA

At the beginning of the 1900s, Great Britain had the world's most powerful navy. Even though World War I was mainly a land war, the Royal Navy ruled the seas. This meant that supplies could be easily carried to support the land army. Having sea power made a country very strong.

DREADNOUGHT

Built in 1906, HMS *Dreadnought* changed warfare at sea forever. It was the fastest and best-armed warship in the world. Its closest rivals did not have half its firepower. It made all other battleships out of date.

BATTLESHIP GIANTS

By the start of World War II in 1939, many countries had produced some awesome battleships. The British navy had HMS *Hood* and HMS *King George V*. The United States had the USS *Iowa* and the USS *North Carolina*. The German navy fought back with the *Bismarck, Scharnhorst,* and *Graf Spee*.

This cruise missile is being fired by a U.S. battleship.

nuclear missile   weapon with huge destructive power

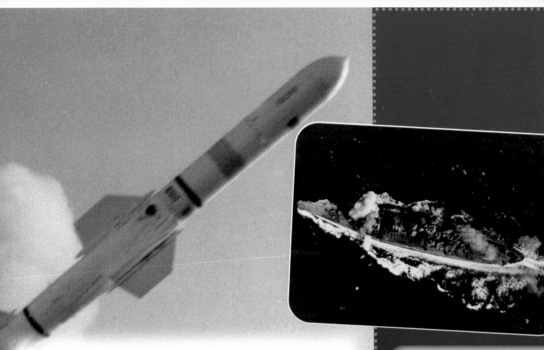

CHANGING ROLES

World War II signaled a change in the role of the battleship. When Japanese planes sank eight U.S. battleships that were docked at Pearl Harbor (in Hawaii) in 1941, it was clear how effective aircraft could be. The days of the great battleships were ending.

A NEW ROLE

The invention of **nuclear missiles** meant that wars could be fought in a different way. Large, expensive battleships were no longer so important. Many were taken out of service and scrapped. Today, battleships no longer fight each other at sea. There are very few left. The firepower of smaller modern ships is much greater, and they can now do the job of the battleships.

JAPANESE GIANT

The Japanese battleship *Yamato* was the largest ever built. Its main guns were the largest to go to sea. Each shell they fired weighed 3,219 pounds (1,460 kilograms), about the weight of a large car. Even though it had more armor than any other ship, the *Yamato* was sunk by U.S. forces in 1945.

FLAT TOPS

The most powerful warships afloat are the huge aircraft carriers, more commonly known as "flat tops."

Aircraft are very important in modern warfare. But for aircraft to be useful, they must have a safe place to take off and land.

TO BOLDLY GO . . .

The first nuclear-powered aircraft carrier was the USS *Enterprise*, launched in 1961. It carries 90 aircraft and has a **crew** of more than 5,500. This super ship can go for fifteen years without having to refuel.

FLOATING AIRPORTS

Aircraft carriers can go anywhere in the world. They act as a base for military operations. Wherever there is a problem, aircraft carriers are usually the first on the scene. **Reconnaissance** aircraft can be launched from their decks. These planes bring back the information that ships' commanders need.

Aircraft carriers can be up to 1,150 ft (350 m) long.

ONE SHIP, MANY JOBS

Aircraft can be launched to attack enemy targets. Because the largest flat tops carry as many as 90 aircraft, these attacks can be devastating. They can cause incredible damage and destruction. Aircraft carriers also launch landing boats filled with troops during invasions.

Aircraft carriers are used for many other operations. They often look after medical helicopters and make sure that troops are kept fully supplied with everything they need. They also defend against air attacks with missiles and helicopters. They even carry special helicopters designed to seek out and destroy **submarines.**

A flat top is also a command center. In times of trouble and danger, the big decisions are made on board.

INSIDE A FLAT TOP

This diagram shows the various sections and parts of a typical aircraft carrier. The hangar is where aircraft are held when not in use. The catapults are used to get the planes traveling at high speeds in order to take off.

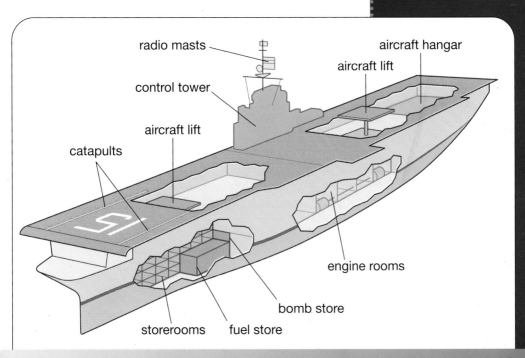

radio masts

aircraft hangar

aircraft lift

control tower

aircraft lift

catapults

engine rooms

bomb store

storerooms   fuel store

HIGH-SPEED NAVY

By far the fastest military boats are the hydrofoils and hovercraft. Both of these are so quick because they sail with their **hulls** above the water.

The advantages of a military hydrofoil are clear. They are much faster than normal ships. Hovercraft are very fast, too, and can be used in many different situations.

JETS

Launched in 1967, the *Tucumcari* was the first hydrofoil to use water jets instead of **propellers**. It was used during the Vietnam War and could travel at around 60 mph (96 km/h).

ANY BEACH, ANYWHERE

Hovercraft are not used far out in open waters. Their main use is around the **coast.** They are used to get troops quickly onto the land. Since hovercraft can operate on land, troops and equipment do not have to be unloaded at the edge of the water.

> ➤ ➤ ➤ ➤ ➤ ➤ ➤ ➤ ➤ ➤
> To find out more about hovercraft, see pages 34–35.

drag (also called water resistance)   force that pushes against a boat and slows it down as it moves through the water

ON PATROL

Smaller hovercraft are excellent coastal and river patrol boats. They are not only used in wartime. They also help in anti-crime operations. They are quick and **maneuverable**. Since they are not just limited to the water, they can patrol the land, too.

The larger assault hovercraft carry huge loads, but still travel at around 50 mph (80 km/h). They are also well armed and can fight off most attackers. This has led to them being nicknamed "hovertanks." Some assault hovercraft have even been used in the middle of the desert.

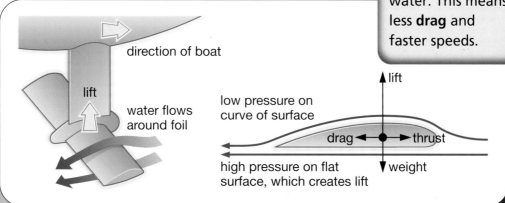

direction of boat

lift

water flows around foil

low pressure on curve of surface

high pressure on flat surface, which creates lift

lift

drag ←→ thrust

weight

Hovercraft are effective on land as well as water.

hull   main body of a ship that sits in the water
maneuverable   able to move and turn easily

INVISIBLE ATTACKER

Surprise is a great weapon in sea warfare. However, ships can be spotted easily by **radar**. The best answer is to design a ship that is hard for radar to see. If a ship is the right shape and covered with the right materials, radar is useless. These "invisible" craft are called **stealth** ships.

TESTING AT SEA

The Lockheed-Martin *Sea Shadow* is a stealth ship. It was originally used to test new technology, but it became clear that its stealth features were the most important. It is now in full service with the U.S. Navy.

DISAPPEARING...

How the *Sea Shadow* becomes "invisible":

- slanted surfaces deflect radar;
- **hull** is made of special material that is hard for radar to see;
- twin hulls create a small **wake** and little noise;
- engines are very quiet.

TECH TALK

Sea Shadow: technical data
- Length: 164 ft (50 m)
- Width: 679 ft (20.7 m)
- Weight: 627 tons
- Crew: 10

radar (Radio Detection And Ranging)   way of detecting things when they are many miles away

SECRET MISSION

The *Sea Shadow* was designed and built in complete secrecy. Parts were made in different places and by different teams of engineers. This was done to keep information about the ship as secret as possible. Even today, only very basic information about this ship can be found.

Sea Shadow is the secret agent of the ship world. It is outstanding at **reconnaissance** missions and avoiding being seen by its enemies.

SILENT AND DEADLY

This Swedish Visby-class ship is built for anti-**submarine** warfare. It is powered by quiet water-jet engines. It has a light **carbon-fiber** hull, making it invisible to radar and **sonar**. All its weapons are inside the hull.

wake   waves that spread out from the back of a ship when it is moving forward

Water covers 71 percent of the earth's surface. Ships have sailed over every part of it. But the ocean beneath the surface is largely unexplored. Even though more than 90 percent of life on our planet lives in the sea, we know very little about it.

DEEPEST DIVE

The deeper you go, the more unexplored the waters become. The deepest place in the world is in the Pacific Ocean. It is called Challenger Deep, after the ship that found it. Mount Everest could sit in Challenger Deep and still be covered with about 1.2 miles (2 kilometers) of water.

Sending **submarines** as deep as this is very difficult and very dangerous.

BATHYSPHERE

Dr. William Beebe invented the Bathysphere in 1930. It was a large metal container that held air, and he used it for diving. He dived to a depth of 3,028 ft (923 m) in it. The previous record was by a diver in an armored suit at just 525 ft (160 m). Beebe explored where no other human had been.

To withstand the pressure of the water, the walls of the Bathysphere were 18 in. (45 cm) thick.

THE DEEPEST EVER

In 1960 the U.S. Navy sent a specially designed mini-submarine to Challenger Deep. It was called the *Trieste*, and two men went down inside it.

At 34,829 feet (10,616 meters) below the surface, the *Trieste* touched the bottom.

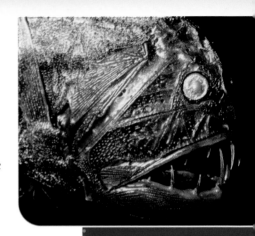

MIGHTY-MINI

The *Trieste* may have been tiny, but it had to be very strong. The deeper a submarine goes, the more water is on top of it. This means that there is a greater pressure pushing down. Imagine how incredibly strong the pressure would be with nearly 7 miles (11 kilometers) of water above you!

The *Trieste* holds the record for the deepest dive to this day. It will continue to hold it unless somewhere deeper is found.

STRANGE FISH

Some very weird creatures live in the deep ocean. Because of the darkness, their eyes are very large. They often have long fangs and look more like creatures from another planet. Some fish can even light up.

air trapped inside

ROBOT WRECK-FINDERS

When ships sink, they go to the bottom of the ocean. Depending on where they are, that can be a long way down. Scientists use amazing technology to find and study shipwrecks.

Scientists use **sonar** to find shipwrecks. Then they send remote **infrared** cameras down to check. The cameras can be "driven" to wherever the operator wants.

The most dangerous and expensive method scientists use to study wrecks is to go down and take a look themselves. This is done in specially designed craft called submersibles. The most famous submersible is called *Alvin*.

DIVING BELLS

Turn a glass upside down and lower it into a bowl of water. The air stays inside the glass. Diving bells work in the same way, but are large enough to contain people. They have been used for centuries. People think the English scientist Roger Bacon invented them in 1250.

infrared   type of light that cannot be seen by the human eye

LOST AND FOUND

This amazing submersible has underwater lights, cameras, and robotic arms to collect samples.

Alvin has had an exciting life so far. In addition to searching for wrecks all over the world, *Alvin* even helped to recover a lost nuclear bomb. But its most famous adventure was finding the *Titanic*, the cruise **liner** that sank in 1912.

TECH TALK

Alvin: technical data
- Length: 23.3 ft (7.1 m)
- Height: 12.1 ft (3.7 m)
- Operating depth: 14,764 ft (4,500 m)
- Crew: 3
- Normal dive length: 6–10 hours
- Maximum life support: 72 hours

UNSINKABLE?

The most famous shipping disaster in history happened in 1912. The luxury cruise liner *Titanic* set off on its maiden voyage to the United States. The proud owners boasted that it was unsinkable. They were wrong. *Titanic* hit an iceberg and hundreds died. This picture of the front of the *Titanic* was taken by *Alvin* more than 70 years after it sank.

maiden voyage   ship's first voyage or journey
sonar   method of detecting where things are under water

Ohio-class submarine:
technical data
- Length: 557.7 ft (170 m)
- Width: 42 ft (12.8 m)
- Top speed: 17 mph (27 km/h) (surface); 29 mph (46.5 km/h) (under water)
- Crew: 160

NUCLEAR SUBS

A nuclear **submarine** is powered by a nuclear reactor. It can stay at sea for very long periods of time, since it does not need to be refueled. Submarines are the original **stealth** ships. They cruise the oceans of the world unseen and carry out a wide range of missions.

FICTION INTO FACT

The first nuclear submarine was the USS *Nautilus*, seen below. It was named after the fictional submarine from Jules Verne's story *20,000 Leagues Under the Sea. Nautilus* was launched in 1954 and soon broke all underwater speed and distance records. In 1958 it was the first ship to reach the North Pole—deep below the surface, of course.

OHIO CLASS

There are at least sixteen of these submarines in service. Each one carries enough nuclear missiles to destroy entire continents.

ballistic missile explosive rocket that has its own engines and can direct itself toward a chosen target

MODERN SUBMARINES

There are two different types of modern submarine.

Attack submarines hunt down and destroy surface ships and other submarines. They can stay under water for years because the air inside them is recycled. They can stay at sea for a long time, so they carry many weapons. This means they do not have to return home to collect more.

The second type is the **ballistic missile** craft. These do not fight other ships, but travel the oceans, staying hidden. When needed, they rise from the seas to launch **nuclear missiles** at an enemy. They are the most deadly fighting machines ever built.

The USS *Nautilus* is now a floating museum in Connecticut.

SHIPPING WORLD

Ships are still the most important way to transport **cargo** around the globe. About 95 percent of all goods travel by boat.

CONTAINERS

Cargo is packed into standard-sized containers. Giant cranes lift the sealed containers straight off the ships onto trucks waiting below. Although this has made cargo handling easier, some ships are so big that some ports cannot cope with them.

GIANT TANKERS

Oil tankers are special ships that carry oil around the world. Without them, the world would not be able to operate the way it does today. Since we use enormous amounts of oil every day, the ships that carry the oil are huge.

ENVIRONMENTAL NIGHTMARE

Oil tankers have a huge environmental responsibility. If things go wrong, there can be a disaster. The tanker above, the *Torrey Canyon*, hit rocks in the English Channel in 1967. The oil spill caused terrible damage to the water and coastline.

stable firm and steady

MONSTER

The Norwegian *Jahre Viking* is the largest ship afloat. This oil tanker is massive. It is so big that it takes several miles for it to slow down and stop.

The *Jahre Viking* is 1,503 feet (458 meters) long. If you could tip the *Jahre Viking* on its end, the ship would be taller than the Empire State Building in New York. In fact, its cargo holds are so big they could swallow up London's St. Paul's Cathedral four times over. If the Eiffel Tower were laid on its side, that would fit in, too.

Each time the *Jahre Viking* goes to sea, it is carrying cargo worth around $150 million. The **crew** of this monster use bicycles to move about on deck.

COMPUTER CONTROL

Ships must be very carefully loaded to keep them **stable**. Cargo is carefully positioned using computers. If the ship does not sit evenly in the water, it may be in trouble once its journey has started.

MEGALINERS

Luxury **liners** had their golden age in the early 1900s. Their main purpose then was taking passengers from one place to another. There are far fewer liners around today. They now take people on luxury cruise vacations.

COMFORT AND STYLE

To take a vacation cruise is many people's idea of the ultimate in luxury. The ships sail to some of the most beautiful and exciting places on Earth. The lucky passengers enjoy all that these amazing luxury **vessels** have to offer.

The best liners have restaurants, theaters, and shopping malls on board. There are even health and beauty clubs and "street cafés." There are many different kinds of entertainment, and there is always something to do or see.

TECH TALK

Voyager of the Seas: technical data
- Length: 1,020 ft (311 m)
- Width: 157.5 ft (48 m)
- Cruising speed: 25 mph (40 km/h)
- Crew: 1,181
- Weight: 151,017 tons
- Passengers: 3,840

VOYAGER OF THE SEAS

When it first set sail in 1999, the *Voyager of the Seas* was the largest cruise ship afloat. This amazing ship has a skating rink, a street fair, and a rock-climbing wall. There is also a casino, theater, movie theater, library, chapel, and several nightclubs. Sports fans can play golf, basketball, volleyball, go scuba diving, or go to the gym. Guests can also eat in a different restaurant every night of their vacation!

FIT FOR A QUEEN

The world's most famous cruise liner is the *Queen Elizabeth II*, or the *QE2* for short. It was first launched in 1969, and even has a branch of the fancy English store Harrods on board.

◄ ◄ ◄ ◄ ◄ ◄ ◄ ◄ ◄ ◄

To find out more about luxury liners, see pages 14–15.

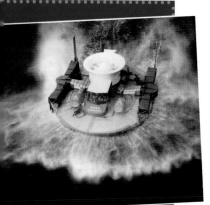

HOVERCRAFT

Hovercraft are ships that float over water and land on a cushion of air. The British scientist Christopher Cockerell invented the hovercraft in 1956.

EARLY DAYS

Cockerell tried out his first ideas using cat food and coffee cans, a huge fan, and some kitchen scales! Some of the early **prototypes** looked very strange. But Cockerell learned that traveling on air could be done.

◄ ◄ ◄ ◄ ◄ ◄ ◄ ◄

To find out more about hovercraft, see pages 20–21.

FIRST TO SUCCEED

The first real working hovercraft was the *SRN1*. Many scientists thought that a hovercraft was possible. But Cockerell's *SRN1* was the first to successfully operate in 1959.

Cockerell's idea went on to become very successful.

prototype   version that is built and tested before the real thing is made

STYLE

As you might expect, no expense is spared inside these amazing boats. Everything is made from top quality materials. These yachts use all of the latest equipment. There is plenty of deck space to soak up the sun and the sights, too!

BUY OR HIRE?

Many companies hire out their luxury yachts for very wealthy people to use for vacations. A private jet picks up vacationers from wherever they choose. Then a luxury car carries them to the harbor. The captain and **crew** are waiting to greet them. If you have many millions of dollars to spare, you could buy your own luxury yacht!

PREDATOR PERFECTION

The outside of the Sunseeker *Predator* is a racing machine, but the inside is a palace. The *Predator* is so expensive that only a few are made each year. Only very rich people can afford to own them.

BREAKING THE ICE

In very cold parts of the world, special ships are needed to break the ice that can form on waterways. These ships are called icebreakers.

Icebreakers do the important job of making sure that ports and harbors stay open in winter. They clear the way for other ships. They can also be used on rescue and exploration missions.

BRUTE FORCE

The early icebreakers were made out of wood. They tried to batter their way through the ice using brute force. Because wood is quite flexible, these ships had some success. But the strength of the ice usually won in the end.

INTELLIGENT DESIGN

Modern icebreakers are computer-designed to help them beat the ice. The **hull** has a stepped design, which helps it to rise above the ice. The whole weight of the ship can then press down like a giant sledgehammer.

The hull of an icebreaker is extremely thick. It is made of special steel that stays strong even at low temperatures. Inside the hull is a skeleton of thick steel ribs. These stop the ice from crushing the ship like a tin can.

BATTERING RAM

The engines of an icebreaker are powerful. Some are even nuclear-powered. They must force the ship up against the ice. Since the engines drive the hull up and forward, gravity does the hard work of smashing the ice.

SEASONAL ICE-SMASHER

The *Botnica* is three ships in one. In summer it can operate as a towboat or as a supply ship. In winter it returns to duty as an icebreaker. It keeps the **coast** and waterways of Finland open for business.

SMALL BOATS

James Bond movies have been thrilling audiences since 1962. They are among the movie world's most popular action-adventure films. All the movies involve Bond in exciting chase scenes. Many of these action-packed chases involve boats.

Since the character of James Bond was a commander in the British Royal Navy, it is only right that many of his adventures should happen on water.

BOND ON THE WATER

In *Thunderball*, Bond chases the *Disco Volante*. This unique ship splits in two during the action to reveal a hydrofoil. There are also amazing underwater action scenes in this movie, using specially designed underwater craft.

AWESOME STUNTS

Live and Let Die includes a spectacular chase scene involving speedboats. The boats jump over roads, hurtle over roadblocks, cut corners by going on dry land, and even gatecrash a wedding party.

This Lotus could travel on land and on water.

gondola   long, narrow, flat-bottomed boat used on canals. It is moved along by pushing on a long pole

SUPER BOATS FOR A SUPER HERO

The Spy Who Loved Me has plenty of action in boats, too. Most famous is the Lotus Esprit **submarine** car that comes straight out of the sea onto a crowded beach. This movie also features the *Liparus*, a tanker that swallows other ships, as well as the sight of Bond on a ski-bike.

In *Tomorrow Never Dies*, Bond has to track down a **stealth** boat to defeat the villain. Once he finds the stealth boat, he must somehow get on board.

Moonraker mixes action with a sense of humor. Bond used a specially equipped **gondola** to get the better of his enemies.

BOND'S BEST?

The "Q boat" (below) is the best-equipped Bond boat so far. In *The World Is Not Enough*, Bond puts it to use on the Thames River. The boat can dive under water and run on land!

43

POWERBOATS

Racing powerboats are designed to win. Speed and strength are more important than comfort or space. There are three main types of powerboat.

HULL DESIGN

Powerboats with a single hull have a narrow, v-shaped **bow**. This hull is designed to rise up on top of the water at high speeds. The hulls are flat underneath so they skim the surface with very little **drag**.

CLASS-1 POWERBOATS

These are the fastest racing boats on the water. Two massive engines take up over half the space of the 5-ton craft. **Crews** of two compete around courses that are about 160 miles (250 kilometers) long. They must make their way around specially placed **buoys** at speeds of up to 150 miles per hour (240 kilometers per hour).

These powerboats are spectacular to watch and very noisy. It is an extremely dangerous sport, so the crew rides inside a **cockpit** as strong as those on fighter jet!

buoy   floating sign or marker that acts as a warning to ships
cockpit   small space in a racing boat where the crew sits

CLASS-2 POWERBOATS

These boats are slightly smaller than Class-1s. They include both single **hulls** and **catamarans.**

The **monohulls** do better in rough conditions, but the catamarans are better in smooth conditions. This is because the catamarans need smooth water to skim across. A monohull cuts through the waves, so smooth conditions are not so important.

CIRCUIT RACERS

Circuit racers are small single-seaters that race around short, tight circuits. There can be as many as 70 laps in a race. Circuit racing takes place close to land, so many people show up to watch.

The cornering is amazing. Sharp turns are taken at over 90 miles per hour (144 kilometers per hour). This puts more pressure on the driver than on a pilot in a fighter jet!

POWER CATS

The two slim hulls of a catamaran cut through water faster than large single hulls. Catamarans roll from side to side less than a monohull. A cushion of air between the hulls lifts the boat, so it looks like it is flying.

monohull ship with a single hull

SUPER-SAIL CRAFT

The fastest sailing craft are the big ocean racers. The **monohull** yachts can cope with the roughest oceans and the strongest winds. The **catamaran** ocean racers can reach higher top speeds.

SAVING WEIGHT

In races or record attempts, it is important to keep weight low. Members of the **crew** only have one set of clothes. The inside of the boat is almost empty, apart from **hammocks** where they sleep. All the food is dried to save weight, and a machine turns seawater into drinking water.

A number of things are required to win races and break records. The yacht must be well designed, strong, and tough. Members of the crew must be experts. Finally, some luck is needed to make sure the wind is helpful.

TECH TALK

Yellow Pages Endeavour: **technical data**
- Weight: 390 lb (177 kg)
- Length: 29.9 ft (9.1 m)
- Width: 29.9 ft (9.1 m)
- Sail height: 36.1 ft (11 m)
- Crew: 2
- Top speed: 53 mph (85 km/h)

hammock   piece of cloth that hangs above the floor, used as a bed

RECORD BREAKER

The catamaran *Club Med* broke many sailing records in 2000. It crossed the Atlantic Ocean in 10 days, 14 hours, 54 minutes, and 43 seconds. That is nearly two days faster than the old record for a wind-powered ship.

Club Med also broke the record for the longest distance sailed in a single day. It traveled 626 miles (1001 kilometers) in 24 hours. The average speed of the yacht was 26 miles per hour (42 kilometers per hour).

TECH TALK

Ocean-racing catamaran: technical data
- Weight: 11 tons
- Length: 88.6 ft (27 m)
- Width: 42.7 ft (13 m)
- Mast height: 101.7 ft (31 m)
- Crew: 11
- Top speed: 40 mph (64 km/h)

ROUND THE WORLD

Every four years, the top ocean-racing yachts take part in the Whitbread Round the World Race. It is the most difficult of all sailing races. The yachts race nearly 32,000 mi (51,200 km). It takes them eight months to finish the race.

WATER-SPEED RECORD

Speed records are there to be broken. People are always trying to be "the fastest." Breaking the water-speed record is very risky, because it is more dangerous to race on water than on land.

THE BLUEBIRD LEGEND

Vehicles called *Bluebird* have held many speed records, on both water and land. In the 1930s, Sir Malcolm Campbell broke nine land-speed records and three water-speed records. Every car or boat he used was called *Bluebird*.

LIKE FATHER, LIKE SON

In 1964 Campbell's son, Donald, followed in his father's footsteps. He broke the land-speed record in Australia. Of course, this 403-mile per hour (648-kilometer an hour) car was called *Bluebird*.

HOME-MADE

Ken Warby broke the water-speed record in 1978 in *Spirit of Australia.* He built it himself using a second-hand airplane engine that he bought for $65. He reached a speed of 317 mph (507 km/h).

This picture was taken seconds before the crash that killed Donald Campell.

SUCCESS, THEN DISASTER

Donald Campbell became the only person to hold land- and water-speed records at the same time. He had achieved something his father did not. But in 1967 he wanted to be the first person to go over 300 mph (480 km/h) on water. He took *Bluebird* to Lake Coniston in England.

Campbell tried to break the record without waiting for waves on the water to settle. As he reached top speed, *Bluebird* hit a wave and lifted out of the water. It spun several times in the air and slammed into the water. Donald Campbell's body was not found until 2001—34 years later.

Sir Malcolm Campbell in *Bluebird K4*.

Find out more about water-speed records on pages 58–59.

SPECIAL SHIPS

SATELLITES FROM THE SEA

Large broadcasting companies or cell phone operators often need to have new satellites put into orbit. They also need to take care of the ones that are already up there.

The Boeing Sea-Launch program is designed to launch rockets into space from the middle of the ocean. These rockets carry **satellites.** Modern technology relies heavily upon satellites circling Earth.

LAUNCHING FROM THE SEA

There are advantages of sending a rocket into space from the ocean. The main one is that the rocket can be launched from the **equator.** This means the rocket will be taking the shortest, most direct route into orbit. Launching satellites this way is also cheaper.

The *Odyssey* arrives at the port of Long Beach on October 4, 1998. The first launch was in March 1999.

equator imaginary line around the middle of Earth, halfway between the north and south poles

LAUNCH PAD

The launch platform is called *Odyssey*. It is similar to an oil rig. It has space for the 68 **crew** members and technicians as well as the rocket and launch system itself. The platform is 436 feet (133 meters) long, 220 feet (67 meters) wide, and weighs more than 55,100 tons.

COMMAND CENTER

The Assembly and Command Ship (ACS) sails around the launch platform. The countdown is controlled from the ACS.

Many successful rocket launches have taken place from the middle of the ocean. Many more will happen in the future.

ROCKETS

Zenit 3SL rockets are used by the Sea-Launch system. They are 197 ft (60 m) long and 13.1 ft (4 m) wide. They use liquid oxygen as a fuel. The different parts of the rocket are made all over the world. They are put together on board the ACS.

satellite   device that circles Earth, sending and receiving signals

WIG BOATS

A WIG boat is a cross between a hovercraft and an aircraft. WIG stands for Wing In Ground-effect. WIG boats skim across the surface of the water at very high speeds. They have been experimental for many years, and no one has quite managed to make them widely used.

GROUND EFFECT

When an aircraft lands, just before touchdown, it seems like the plane does not want to go lower. Air becomes trapped between the wing and the runway, forming an air cushion. A WIG boat uses this cushion to ride upon.

The problem has been that WIG boats need to reach high speeds to make this effect happen.

NEW MONSTER?

The aircraft maker Boeing is designing a new WIG boat. Although little is known about this craft, it is said to be bigger than the Caspian Sea Monster. It will probably be used for carrying **cargo**. When it travels at 23 ft (7 m) above the water it should reach 300 mph (480 km/h).

CIA (Central Intelligence Agency) U.S. government agency set up to gather information about potential enemies

THE CASPIAN SEA MONSTER

The largest WIG craft ever built was the giant Russian *Ekranoplan*. It was very secret and was first learned about by the **CIA** in the 1960s. They nicknamed it the Caspian Sea Monster.

Ekranoplan was more than 301 feet (92 meters) long. It was designed as a military **vessel** for carrying between 800 and 900 soldiers. It could reach speeds of 345 miles per hour (552 kilometers per hour), even though it weighed 540 tons. This was twice the weight of the heaviest aircraft at the time. To get up enough speed to leave the surface of the water, *Ekranoplan* had ten engines.

ORLYONOK

The *Orlyonok* is a **prototype** designed to become a military transport craft. Early tests were successful, but the project was put on hold in 1993. New interest in WIG machines means that the *Orlyonok* may fly/sail again.

The *Ekranoplan* project was scrapped in the 1980s after a crash.

53

WEIRD IDEAS

Many strange boat designs have appeared over the years. Not all of them have been successful. Here are just a few.

FIRE AND WATER

Fire ships are an unusual but successful idea. They are really just floating fire engines, able to tackle fires on ships or close to rivers or ports. The **hull** of a fire ship has special pumps that suck in water. Hoses spray this water all over the fire. A fire ship has a nearly endless supply of water.

THE FLIP SHIP

FLIP is a weird research ship. It has doors in the floor, windows in the ceiling, tables bolted to walls, and stairs that lead nowhere.

This is because *FLIP* lives up to its name. It flips on its end so only a small part is left above the surface. The weird design means that most of the ship is below the waves. This provides scientists with a much more **stable** place to carry out their research than on a bobbing ship. The waves have less effect because the ship is so well balanced under water.

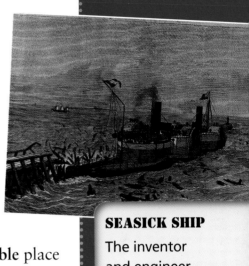

SEASICK SHIP

The inventor and engineer Henry Bessemer designed a ship he hoped would cure his seasickness. The idea was to produce a platform that would always be stable, no matter how rough the sea was. It was a disaster and sank on its first voyage.

Fires on board tankers can be disastrous.

FUTURE BOATS

So what does the future hold for the world of boats?

Although boats have been built for thousands of years, people are still producing new boat designs, new engines, and improved building materials. The ideas never seem to run out.

SHAPING THE FUTURE

The Russian navy has developed a rocket-powered torpedo called the Shkval. It can travel at five times the speed of a normal torpedo, over 300 miles per hour (480 kilometers per hour). This makes it very difficult to stop.

The torpedo runs so fast because it produces millions of small bubbles around its nose. These bubbles reduce the **friction,** so a higher speed is reached with the same amount of power. Adding a rocket engine helps, too!

SUPERSONIC SUB?

Scientists hope that ideas from the Shkval torpedo could produce a supersonic submarine one day. They intend to surround a submarine with a giant bubble. This would remove most of the underwater **drag,** allowing very high speeds.

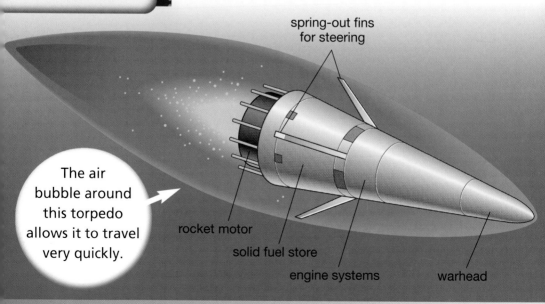

spring-out fins for steering

The air bubble around this torpedo allows it to travel very quickly.

rocket motor

solid fuel store

engine systems

warhead

NEW DESIGNS, NEW IDEAS

The technology used to design the Shkval torpedo could also be used to build super-fast **submarines**. Perhaps in the future, it will be quicker to travel under the water than on the surface.

UNDERWATER FLYING

Deep Flight is a brand new submarine design. Normal submarines rely on letting air in and out to dive and rise to the surface. A hot-air balloon rises and falls in a similar way. *Deep Flight* does not have to do this. Small wings allow the sub to "fly" around the ocean. *Deep Flight* can change direction or depth without letting air in or out.

FASTER AND FASTER

Normal ships have a long, thin **stern** that sinks into the water. A new design called *FastShip* (above) has a wide, hollow stern. This means *FastShip* lifts up at the back and moves faster. Water jets give the ship its power.

---

stern back end of a boat or ship

BOAT FACTS

Water-speed record highlights				
			Speed	
Date	Driver	Vehicle	km/h	mph
1928	George Wood	Miss America VII	149.3	92.8
1930	Henry Segrave	Miss England II	159.0	98.8
1931	Gar Wood	Miss America IX	164.4	102.2
1937	Malcolm Campbell	Bluebird K3	203.2	126.3
1939	Malcolm Campbell	Bluebird K4	228.0	141.7
1950	Stanley Sayres	Slo-Mo-Shun IV	258.0	160.3
1955	Donald Campbell	Bluebird K7	325.6	202.3
1959	Donald Campbell	Bluebird K7	419.1	260.4
1967	Lee A. Taylor	Hustler	459.0	285.2
1978	Ken Warby	Spirit of Australia	511.1	317.6

Largest cruise ships		
Ship	Weight (tons)	Passengers
Queen Mary 2	156,749	2,800
Explorer of the Seas	151,356	3,840
Adventure of the Seas	151,320	3,840
Mariner of the Seas	151,320	3,840
Navigator of the Seas	151,320	3,807
Voyager of the Seas	151,320	3,840
Diamond Princess	124,561	2,600
Sapphire Princess	124,561	3,100
Carnival Conquest	121,517	3,783
Carnival Glory	121,254	3,783
Carnival Valor	121,254	3,783
Crown Princess	121,254	3,100

Worst oil tanker spills		
Tanker	Date	Spillage (tons)
Atlantic Empress	July 1979	316,400
ABT Summer	May 1991	286,600
Castillo de Bellver	August 1983	277,800
Amoco Cadiz	March 1978	245,800
Haven	April 1991	158,700
Odyssey	November 1988	145,500
Torrey Canyon	March 1967	131,200
Sea Star	December 1972	126,800
Irenes Serenade	February 1980	110,200
Urquida	May 1976	110,200

Blue Riband holders		
Ship	Date	Time
Sirius	1838	18 days, 14 hours, 22 minutes
Great Western	1838	12 days, 16 hours, 24 minutes
Persia	1856	8 days, 23 hours, 19 minutes
Kaiser Wilhelm	1897	5 days, 17 hours, 23 minutes
Mauretania	1909	4 days, 10 hours, 51 minutes
Queen Mary	1938	3 days, 20 hours, 42 minutes
United States	1952	3 days, 10 hours, 40 minutes
Hoverspeed Great Britain	1990	3 days, 7 hours, 54 minutes
Catlink IV	1998	2 days, 20 hours, 9 minutes

The most expensive ticket on the **maiden voyage** of the Queen Mary 2 in January 2004 cost $37,499.

There were 3,547 passengers on the Titanic when it sank in 1912. There were only enough lifeboats for 1,178 people.

FIND OUT MORE

BOOKS

Dorling Kindersley Publishing Staff. *Eyewitness: Submarines*. New York: DK, 2003.

Graham, Ian. *Ships and Submarines*. Danbury, Conn: Franklin Watts, 2000.

Loves, June. *Ships*. Broomall, Penn: Chelsea House, 2001.

WORLD WIDE WEB

If you want to find out more about boats, you can search the Internet using keywords such as these:

- "**yacht** racing"
- powerboat + race
- luxury + yacht
- *Titanic*
- tanker + disaster

Make your own keywords using headings or words from this book. The search tips opposite will help you find the most useful websites.

ORGANIZATIONS

USS NAUTILUS

The website for the museum based in Connecticut. Photos of the inside of the first nuclear **submarine** and details of its history.

ussnautilus.org

HMS VICTORY

This site gives a clear idea of what it was like to live on an 18th-century warship.

hms-victory.com

SEARCH TIPS

There are billions of pages on the Internet, so it can be difficult to find exactly what you want to find. If you just type in "boat" on a search engine such as Google, you will get a list of millions of web pages. These search skills will help you to find useful websites more quickly:

- Use simple keywords, not whole sentences.
- Use two to six keywords in a search.
- Be precise—only use names of people, places, or things.
- If you want to find words that go together, put quote marks around them—for example, "world-speed record."
- Use the advanced section of your search engine.
- Use the "+" sign between keywords to find pages with all these words.

GLOSSARY

assembly putting together different parts

ballistic missile explosive rocket that has its own engines and can direct itself toward a chosen target

Blue Riband award given to the ship that crosses the Atlantic Ocean the fastest

bow front end of a boat or ship

buoy floating sign or marker that acts as a warning to ships

carbon fiber very light and very strong building material

cargo goods carried by a ship

catamaran boat with two hulls

CIA (Central Intelligence Agency) U.S. government agency set up to gather information about potential enemies

crankshaft part of an engine that is joined to the pistons. It turns the up-and-down motion of the pistons into a circular motion.

coast where the land meets a large body of water

cockpit small space in a racing boat where the crew sits

crew group of people that works on a boat or ship

cylinder tube-shaped part of an engine in which fuel is burned

drag (also called water resistance) force that pushes against a boat and slows it down as it moves through the water

dry dock special harbor in which ships can be kept out of water

equator imaginary line around the middle of the earth, halfway between the north and south poles

friction force that acts when two things rub together

gondola long, narrow, flat-bottomed boat used on canals. It is moved along by pushing on a long pole

hammock piece of cloth that hangs above the floor of a boat, used as a bed

hull main body of a ship that sits in the water

infrared type of light that cannot be seen by the human eye

liner big ship that carries passengers all over the world

maiden voyage ship's first voyage or journey

maneuverable able to move and turn easily

mast upright pole to which sails are attached

monohull ship with a single hull

nuclear missile weapon with huge destructive power

piston part of an engine that slides in and out of a cylinder

propeller part of a ship's engine that spins under water and drives the ship along

prototype version that is built and tested before the real thing is made

radar (Radio Detection And Ranging) way of detecting things when they are many miles away

reconnaissance finding out information about an enemy

rivet short metal pin that fixes sheets of metal together

sailor member of a ship's crew

satellite device that circles the earth, sending and receiving signals

sonar (Sound and Navigation Ranging) method of detecting where things are under water

stable firm and steady

stealth taking an action secretly or quietly; in boats, a vessel constructed so that it does not show up on radar

stern back end of a boat or ship

submarine ship that can travel under water

vessel another word for a ship or boat

wake waves that spread out from the back of a ship when it is moving forward

welder person who joins pieces of metal by melting the edges

yacht large boat used for pleasure cruising or racing

Raintree would like to thank the following for information used in the book:
Lloyd's Register – Fairplay Ltd
ITOPF Ltd

INDEX